Egyptian Compass

Egyptian Compass

Poems by Pauline Kaldas

CustomWords

Published by CustomWords
P.O. Box 541106
Cincinnati, OH 45254-1106

Typeset in Garamond by WordTech Communications LLC,
Cincinnati, OH

ISBN: 1933456256
LCCN: 2006925212

Poetry Editor: Kevin Walzer
Business Editor: Lori Jareo

Visit us on the web at www.custom-words.com

Cover photograph: "Alexandria in My Eyes," Ayman El-Kharrat
Author photograph: Lorraine Chittock/*Saudi Aramco World*/PADIA

Acknowledgments

Grateful acknowledgment is made to the following publications for publishing these poems or earlier versions of them:

Anthology of Arab American and Anglophone Arab Literature, ed. Nathalie Handal: "I am Born in Egypt," "Veiled," "Back" (2007).
Borderlands: Texas Poetry Review: "Some Woman Try to Run Me Down," "Back Porch" (2001).
Contemporary Arab American Poetry, ed. Hayan Charara: "Bird Lessons," "Fraudulent Acts," "My Aunt's Kitchen," "What America Has to Offer" (2007).
Contemporary Voices of the Eastern World: An Anthology of Poems, eds. Tina Chang, Nathalie Handal, and Ravi Shankar: "Cairo Walk" (2007).
Cultural Activisms: Poetic Voices, Political Voices, eds. Gertrude Gonzalez and Anne Mamary: "In Line, Waiting," "In the Park," "Bird Lessons" (1999).
A Different Path: Anthology of the Radius of Arab American Writers, eds. D.H. Melhem and Leila Diab: "In the Park," "Morning"(2000).
Egyptian Diary, music composed by T. J. Anderson Jr.: "Back,""Streets are Endless Configurations," "A Visit" (1991).
Food for Our Grandmothers: Writings by Arab-American and Arab-Canadian Feminists, ed. Joanna Kadi: "Exotic," "ABC/ ا ب ت" (1994).
International Quarterly: "Egypt, the War of 1967," "Home" (1994).
Lift: "Garbage City," "Elegy for a Man Walking on Kasr el Aini Street," "Veiled," "Cairo Walk" (1992), "Back," "Streets are Endless Configurations" (1991), "Exotic," "The Roof Crumbles," "ABC/ ا ب ت" (1990).
Michigan Quarterly Review: "Bird Lessons" (1992).
Mizna: "A House in Old Cairo," "Utterances," "Homelands Amiss" (2006), "Inquiry for a Birth Certificate," "Egyptian Goddess Paperweight," "Rubies," "Skyfall" (2003), "What America Has to Offer," "My Aunt's Kitchen" (1999).
Phoebe: "Leap to Grasp," "Mosaic" (2000).
The Poetry of Arab Women: A Contemporary Anthology, ed. Nathalie Handal: "Morning," "Home" (2001).

Post-Gibran: *Anthology of New Arab American Writing*, eds. Khaled
      Mattawa and Munir Akash: "Fraudulent Acts," "From A
      Distance Born" (1999).
So to Speak: "Mediterranean Beach" (2000).
The Space Between Our Footsteps, ed. Naomi Shihab Nye: "Home" (1998).

Author's Note

I express my greatest appreciation and respect to T. J. Anderson III from whom I have learned the most about poetry and who has had the greatest impact on my work. As my harshest critic, he pushed me to go further with poetry than I could have ever imagined.

My deep thanks goes to Milton Kessler, Ruth Stone, Jeffner Allen, and Susan Strehle, at Binghamton University, whose advice, encouragement, and love of poetry enabled me to bring this manuscript into existence.

I extend my appreciation to Lisa Suhair Majaj, a friend and fellow writer for many years whose understanding of my work made it possible to conceive of myself as an Arab American writer.

Many thanks to all those who have supported my work in various ways: Michelle Abate, Chiji Akoma, T. J. and Lois Anderson, Alyssa Antonelli, Dona Antonelli, Maggie Awadalla, Marcia Douglas, Michael Franco, Jeff Goodman, Nathalie Handal, Julie Haurykiewicz, Sunni Kessler, Ayman Al Kharrat, Rachel MacKnight, Khaled Mattawa, Naomi Shihab Nye, Mona Sarkiss, Joseph and Molly Torra, Ellen Witt, and all my colleagues at Hollins University.

Also, I am grateful to Carole Oles, my first poetry teacher, who was kind enough to encourage me to continue writing.

Finally, I thank my family in America and in Egypt who continually inspire my writing.

for Yasmine and Celine

Contents

I

A B C / أ ب ت

for Yasmine and Celine

Child, open your dark eyes
follow your brown skin to this sound

خ __

        deep from your throat
              bring it out like phlegm

   ع   — in the center below your heart
        pull to a tone like a cymbal

as your grandparents choked their last
  Arabic signature   bought
you a ticket to America

   ح   —walk in a desert
           till your thirst becomes sand

    ه   —walk longer till the air feels of water

like your great grandmother's face melting into the sweat
  from her hand pushing the dough   down   to rise

   ق   —begin to swallow your tongue

your orphan great grandfather died
taking in a breath   rubbing
   the pain in his arm

ث __

       hold your tongue in your teeth
           snatch the air

Mosaic

"You were speaking sad," my daughter says, tears gathering
in her breath. How could she catch my tone so easily, mention
of my grandmother, tucked her name inside my daughter's as if
for safekeeping from forgetting of time that extends with distance
of traveled land, history in two countries, holding the balance
of glaciers breaking, water congeals over ripple flattening.

*

to heal my childhood traumas
my grandmother made me sandwiches
on syrian bread
pressed down white cheese
and peeled slices of cucumbers
to moisten my mouth

*

my aunt locking herself in to study
and I given firm finger shaking instructions
not to disturb her
I'd knock on the door
"Is that you," she'd ask
"No, I'm a watermelon," I say
and through closed door
we'd argue over my identity

*

a piano my grandmother played
in our fanciful Salon room
that I dribbled my fingers on
astounded at the possibility of sound

*

my grandmother standing over a bowl of dough in the kitchen
summer's heat into sweat watching drops slide down her face
her hand turning the dough over and under

*

Jesus crosses that lit up neon in the dark
to mark the distance of my night vision

*

Rita who gave birth
under the terrace stairs
puppies scurrying about her nippled stomach

*

opening the shutters
body leans to overlook street
a man selling *teen el shoki*
prickly pears
he balances between thumb and forefinger
to peel the thorns
offer mouthful of seeds congregating inside red sweet

*

summer evenings   heat subsides with the water's breath cooling us
on our balcony we eat   watermelon & white cheese
salt like a bee sting on my tongue   the melon a sea wave crashing
seeds spit into my fist   like whispered secrets

*

grapeleaves we'd stuff together
around the kitchen table
once a leaf on my plate
with an unusual shape
angles straight at the side
they exclaimed at its strange beauty
I said it's just folded
no no that is its shape they insisted
and when they weren't looking
I unfolded its edge
feeling I had betrayed a miracle

Egypt, the War of 1967

"Tafoo el noor!"
"Tafoo el noor!"
He cries to the people
as he walks through the streets at dusk,
his lantern playing shadows
from houses to sidewalks
and behind him every home
enters the color of night.
The swing of his hand shapes a flat
invisible land as he carries
the blackness into this ancient city.

"Yala! Yala!"
My grandmother rounds us
with her cries.
I touch the chip
in the wall,
lean to the arm
of the chair,
reach the single circle of five.

In this corridor insulated by rooms,
we hold hands.
The white candle glimmers our faces
while the echo of the night
crier is still in our hearing.
We blow the flame silent
and listen for the planes droning above us.
The target is any single glimmer.
My eyes probe this deepest darkness.
I cannot see the outline of a shadow.

"Noor! Noor!"
I'm afraid of the light that will come.

Inquiry for a Birth Certificate

A line in a dusty ledger
spells my four names:
    first name, father's name, grandfather's, great grandfather's
    pulls me descending, almost
            trembling off the page

The line extends in columns:
    birth date, place, mother, father, religion
    If born a day earlier,
    my entry would have been on a previous page
        pieces torn and taped
            fan shaped folds
      one corner absent

                I imagine ledgers in agony, grumbling
                pages repeating in flames
                the letters in my name singed into sparks

Only this record in handwritten script keeps me
with its residue of truth.
In an old immigrant passport
identity is opaqued: space for only three names
one too burdensome for the dotted line.

In the Cairo Airport

The line of people wavers
unsteady from the still heat
held tight within the walls.
Light sifts around corners,
shapes edge forward
towards the glassed officer.
Most have changed their clothes.
Now they stand:
Men in crisp folded suits,
dark stripes.
One man's pants, navy blue,
travel the length of his leg
to caress the bottom of his shoe.
Floor dust marks an outline
around the cuffs.
Women in pastel stockings,
outfits to reflect
this summer's fashion color:
a bright salmon.
One woman styled her hair upwards
but the day's heavy heat
weighs down on it.
As the line holds still,
she rests her smile.

A House in Old Cairo

I
Seeing the house here, no longer imagined
second floor now fallen rubble
the shop below still there
where my grandfather bought us sugarcane juice.
If my great grandfather could survive the train
rolling over him, this house can withstand
the collapse of the second floor.

II
Basket roped down to capture four pigeons and a kilo of potatoes
cooked in the kitchen with a stove, the oven a two block walk.

Only I see sense in my cousin's mother—
captured like pigeons
let out only with male escorts
except on church days, she returns with a shopping bag,
an occasion to comment and she is forgiven
her pride in making cookies.
The cookies are hard her husband says
and his own stiffness with her
as if he never learned to map her body dance.
Now menopause, after four births, two dead
and one miscarriage
he blames her jumping off a chair while hanging laundry,
a moment of ecstasy.

III
What does it matter
my uncle with his cataract eyes
his unforgiving for those who left
believing they could return here,
live like kings.

IV

My father ran from that house
bought a bicycle to run faster
a Fiat on wheels, as far as he could
married my mother,
cutting patterns to imitate
European designs, her smile poised
nineteen year old dreams.
They pulled each other
to pretend the richness true in America.

V

In 1976 we return
and the old house is the same:
my uncle sitting nearest the door
his wife to his left
my grandmother serving mint tea in the same glasses.
When the house began to fall, they had to move
except Korolos, my grandfather's brother
who begged to stay
underneath in the only floor.
They wouldn't let me visit him
too much dirt and no bathroom
for the niece from America.

VI

This house built by my great grandfather Kaldas
run over by a train, survived with all his broken ribs.
His stubbornness and his name we carried over seas
leaving behind my grandfather in the house alone
waiting for his daughter visiting us in America.
He crossed off the calendar days
to the last one
dying the day she returned.

VII
And now that Uncle Korolos died
the house will want another tenant or it may fall
but it will not let go
Kaldas's surviving children,
Korolos the last to insist on living
in this home's final crumbling.

A Visit

The door opens
my aunt wields me to offerings at her altar table
a prayer to heal her son
Cana's wine is a glass of holy water
sprinkled with dipped parsley
incense revels in her house
tuned to my cousin's refrain

Bring me Mariam
I want to marry Mariam

his nerves have blossomed like ivy
twirled into the stripes on his pajamas
teased him to follow the ring in his ear

Bring me Mariam
I will marry Mariam

a personal box
neat arrangement
tucked layers of medicine

He turns to face us
a suspended audience

This cane belonged to Kaldas, my great grandfather
He never let it push into the ground
Otherwise people would think he was weak, could not walk
He held it, like this, in the middle
Balance seesaw, parallel to his body

some numbness around the eye
a tug at the right shoulder
his body deposits to the bed
a half circle turned in to catch the reprise

My Aunt's Kitchen

Cupboard open to rows of glass jars, wax paper lines the lids to close tightly, filled with pickled lemons, beets, peppers, onions; tangerine jam, date jam, grape jam; old cheese in mixture of oil and lemon marinates its taste more pungent daily. Every day, filling clay olas with water, saving empty jars on one side and on the other their mismatched lids to fit later. My uncle's house laid out neatly. He tells me: one side for winter, enclosed porch, no windows look east and light through screens enters heavily; the other side a summer porch, screens unobstructed look over the house of the man who owns *Kentucky Fried Chicken*; in his garden, a young servant girl, hair kerchiefed, follows a dog.

What America Has to Offer

How wonderful this thing they call the supermarket:
cans of fruit salad and pineapple,
graham cracker cookies, frozen vegetables,
dried onions and garlic, canned tomato paste!
Those hours spent washing, cutting, peeling vegetables,
making tomato sauce from tomatoes. Only
a can, poured into a pot, a little water
and you were done?

This is indeed America, the land of miracles.
The men declare: it doesn't taste the same;
they want the long hot day, peeling and chopping
onions and garlic, frying, the smell of *taelia*
to greet them when they come home.

Let them feed themselves.
And the women begin to share secrets
on the back of cake mixes.

Home

The world map
colored yellow and green
draws a straight line from Boston to Cairo.

Homesick for the streets
unkempt with crowds
of people, overfilled so you must
look to put your next step down;
bare feet and galabiyas pinch
you into a spot tighter
than a net full of fish,

drivers bound out
of their hit cars
to battle in the streets
and cause a jam as mysterious
as the building of the pyramids,

sidewalk cafes with overgrown men
heavy suited, play backgammon
and bet salaries from absent jobs,

gypsies lead their carts
with chanting voices
tempting with the smell of crisp fried falafel
and cumin spiced fava beans,

sweetshops
display their baklava and basboosa
glistening with syrup
browned like the people who make them,

women, hair and hands henna red
their eyes, kohl-lined and daring.

The storms gather from the ground
dust and dirt mixed into the sand
a whirlwind flung into my eyes,

I fly across
and land—
hands pressing into rooted earth.

II

I Am Born in Egypt

for Yasmine

Mommy what kind of Arabic do we speak?

Your birth in nativeland
sifting August heat   your weight inside me
I walk Cairo's steamed streets   cross under bridges
                    weave through midday traffic horns
            trail the Nile like a line marking distances
                        one felucca's sail set against the breeze

Labor induced   breathe through
                squat kneel lean into a mosaic shattering
your head stubborn against every move
one arm a rolling pin over my abdomen
                    and the doctor's pull stretch
collapsed into anesthesia
                born into distance
clean wrapped baby   skylight morning

One week old
carrying you to New York's airport   I trip
                catch my landing on one knee
what I have brought
my own loss
        rhythm of sun and wind refrains
                                    seawaves
                                    offering corals

Two years old
we fly back to Egypt
show you off
            fen manakheeric point to nose
but faces waver   the elusiveness of
            prickle sweet sugarcane juice
      junk man's cry   *rubikya!*
months after our return you pick up a bag, step from
dining room to living room and say "I'm going to Egypt"

You eat *ful* with me from the same bowl
learn to catch beans with bread
the Yasmine flower grows only in warm desertland
 but the preschool returns you to me in fluent English

4th birthday child grown
how will you come home?
"Speak the other way Mommy"
making sounds trailing to rhythms
      with each utterance   I pull you closer
                              we tug
like Mediterranean waves reach for shore
                        cutting across the Nile's mud

Morning

for Chiji Akoma

as if words could shed their skin
left bare skimming the air with "good morning"
between me and another walker
cold air striking our faces
entangled in other greetings:

Sabah el kheir
    Sabah el fol
Morning of luck
    Morning of jasmine

Sabah el noor
    Sabah el eshta
Morning of light
    Morning of cream

call and response
syllables carried bring jasmine to my breath
    the voweling of light pulling me to the day

here, the winter language
disconnects bare trees, morning air
and a deer's staring

mumbled so the "good" disappears
only "morning" left
as if to assure ourselves that
this is where we are

not even a mouthful of sounds
stopping me long enough

Bird Lessons

"You will find it in the soup"
 the bowl with steam turning to clouds
into shapes   My friends cringe as they fish
with their spoon net
  but no petals of flesh are caught
          only pilaf noodles that narrow on each end
"We call them bird's tongue because of the shape
 you will find them in the soup"
Their eyes look down
  they had expected something exotic
    and would have preferred pink flesh

but it is I who cringe
    we are not savages   I am blind
by pink tongues flapping in my broth

pink tongues flapping in my broth they paddle to stay alive propel from
one side to the other what if they jump and flap a slap across my face? I
put them in boiling broth expand them to their greatest potential they
are noodles and I am obsessed with their name why should pasta tamer
than alphabets have such a vicious name? the bird left with gaping
hoarse beak put up your fists you phrase maker we have letters to settle I
grew up with my grandmother putting them in my vegetable soup my
mother in chicken soup and I in clear broth how dare you give a name
with color shall giants cut my tongue to flavor their soup and do men
who turn cannibal eat the round soft point you touch the tip of your
nose with? what kind of tongue do the dead have thin flat or with zigzag
cuts like my last lover? how to treat these noodles in my broth will they
grow to giants *lesan el asfour lesan* tongue *el* of *asfour* bird a tiny bird
forced to put in my soup explain to dinner guests what is in their bowls
or when I send a stranger to shop no other translation and I am blind
with birds flapping in my broth.

At the Egyptian Grocery Store

unbalanced   rhythm slips out
discordant in translation
stepping into phonetic English

words fail his showmanship
fencing with another Arab
parrying in tilted tongue

to impress his American wife:
rolls backthroat
swallows gutted arabic script

After Church

He stands alone
so no one will be bothered
by the twitchings of his mouth.

Tell me, do you lose
the words you do not speak?

"What is there to eat," you asked
standing in line to receive
something other than the body and blood.
"You're fasting," your wife
said, "there's nothing to eat."
And you held out your hand
with only two dimes from your pocket
asking for coffee with powdered milk
because fasting means to cleanse yourself
from the animal. She turned from you
and you looked at your hand
but twenty cents could not give you the words.

Skyfall

Once lustrous sculptures from the sky descended
hard pellets insistent

> I cupped my hand:
> one dropped
> like a walnut
> in the scoop of my palm
> its edges bit my skin
> till I let it fall

Standing on the balcony I shouted to ask
what was falling
"Taleg" my mother said.
I stumbled the word up "like the ice cubes in our refrigerator?"
My mother half nodded
Years before I could frame the image with *snow sleet hail*

Antics

Crack a joke
the fine tune of 4th graders' laughter
and I pick up
a half note later
in rhythm

Humor is the last accent you will master
after *ing* silent
after *th* between teeth
get the punch line
citizenship granted

Till then—pretend
catch the edge of the first laugh

In the Park

*"That's why I want to learn to speak
the English...so people will think I'm white."*
                    Zakia, an Ethiopian refugee
                    hoping to come to the U.S.

Gone astray the morning how
landed in sunshine, a dog barked the night
fear mixes slowly like butter and sugar
shaped flat ground into "but your English is so good"
                tongues wounding around loose leaf tepee
                Babel is nonsensical if you're monolingual
                while others gossip about passersby

The Egyptian driver lassoed by his own tongue's swear
when the other boomeranged back the same dialect

                caught by surprise
a stranglehold that tips us to precarious balance
Such a pleasant conversation— slipped out, pulled beneath
unawares the "but you speak English so well"
        like a native— stutter the letters
                sound out the microphone—
a cutthroat tongue frantic

As a child I made up my own language with fingers
tapping the rhythm of syllables
                combining sounds...
We create a tug   *tafrazeehea   tagrageehea*
syntax askew: fingertips play thumb piano melodies
                strutting the harmony alone

Please state your native tongue: misplaced the original
replaced by one non-native

Chattering sounds in one alphabet close
the vowels of your misconstrued remark.

III

Exotic

Dark   your hair is the soil
       eyes lined with the dye of an olive
            your walk is the wind that moves a palm tree

Here,   dark woman
       I will leave my golden beauty
               and take you
who are also permitted:

"Hey girl, how you doin'?"
       "¿Qué pasa niña?"
    "Hey baby!"
"What are you—Lebanese, Armenian, Spanish,
                Puerto Rican, Italian, Mexican,
       c'mon what are you?"
    "You are either Spanish or Italian."

The square edges me
       as it extends *White*
       includes people from North Africa and the Middle East

White?
       as fava beans stirred green with olive oil
       falafel fried sesame seeds burned black
       baklava and basboosa the aroma browned crisp in the oven

White is not my breasts growing at nine
       not the gang of fifth grade boys hurling snowballs
           cornering me to the side of my house

I will draw four sides
contain my X in the box and write my name next to it

for food, pronounce guttural *kha* script
twirl into **ABC**   found in the exotic section
for body, untwirl lengths of cloth

                                       mummy encased in glass

taste a color not confined
by the squares

In Line, Waiting

"I love your shirt.
I love Egyptian!
I love it!!!"

The pharaohs on my shirt
must have struck
him eloquent.
This youth bounding through CVS
without losing a step
announced his views on my native land.
Inspired by Isis
her winged arms outstretched in a gesture

He felt
he must

declare...

Love

    the old city of Cairo   a barefoot boy in white shorts
races with a stick tapping a bicycle tire
a man, his face obscured in a steam of hot clouds, pushes a cart
full of roasting peanuts   5 piasters each soiled brown bag

    a walk on the corniche   turquoise Nile glass blue
as the sun drowns its rays
and the last taxi honks

Shall I say I love your Plymouth Rock and Salem Harbor shirt
    and by such I love American?

sea legs balancing on rock
first crops stagnant in the earth

From your lips this melting pot
compressed image on my back

Egyptian Goddess Paperweight

The head of the Goddess,
layered in 24-kt gold,
stands out on an attractive marble base.
Discount Price: $1.99

Buy your own Goddess
Never mind which one

If it is Tefnut, supporter of the sky,
            disrupted dreams are whisked away.
             As you break from the sheets,
            she receives you
            like the new-born sun.
If Nut, no need to make funeral arrangements.
            She embraces you,
            stretches out her starry body.
If Hathor, always have a dance partner.
            The lyre of song intoxicates,
            decorated with garlands
            you swing and whirl into her music.

Discount Goddess: send your check today!
This silhouetted face protects your papers.

                    but beneath the lamplight
                    Hathor becomes Sekhmet
                    the lioness woman
                    saying
              "when I slay men my heart rejoices"

Bread

for Katz

My roommate asks me to buy bread.
I oblige
carrying home round thin loaves.
Proud I had remembered,
I offer her a pile
sniff of fresh flour.
Her shoulders sigh:
"Just once couldn't you bring home normal bread?"

In My Travels

Only the Indians notice me
they stretch their eyes
       till I must smile
One stops me on the street
with an insistent are you Indian?
       no no
But you must be   never mind you are
no one else speaks to me
       so I shop only in the Indian store
       live on Mango ice cream
This one continues to talk
tells me about the food we eat
       shall I tell him my name?

Some Woman Try to Run Me Down

grinning face   masquerade assaults
                 swerved into entering sidewalk

railroad tracks body laid down
swing low sweet chariot
high over your hooded car

passing my dented frame   my daughter at your wheel's edge
                 silhouetted baby in stroller

What did you see?
     a black woman
   accented refugee
migrant wife

wide arching grin split your skull
     numbed me
looking up to see your face daggered

staking the streets
high above sunglory your mighty head
     nothing blocking your way
             to turn me into
speeding up   your foot down low hit hard a carcass to hang

a child next to you
  your wheel skimming her face

IV

Back

not at all
homesick   outside inside   where
want to be home   here

It won't work   streets stench
                        choking on an intake of breath – fumes from
                                            unfiltered cars
a truck trails gray smoke
                    turns into the dust shade
                    cumulates   on buildings
                    on cars on clothes
                    on hair: grime striped between comb teeth

Once I saw a man cleaning a curved roof, chimney black
his brush left an ivory streak

Every morning speed down broken sidewalks
    you must smell
                        tangled sewers   creeping out of alley streets
this early
taamia frying in sesame bubbling oil
                            taste an aroma streaming
breakfast   —lunch and dinner—
enough of home   not this stench for memory
gas fumes, coughing out carbon monoxide phlegm
breathe this city

Returning by metro down the stairs to this alley way
people clapping singing, a band of bagpipes
bride and groom poised
their wedding witnessed by me and the three women
on the second story balcony in pink flowered nightgowns and curlers

No space for nostalgia
in the two boys riding on yellow milk crates
back home my cousin has a toy car with a real engine

No romance in Rasha
taking small steps in Maadi
holding the naked torso of a doll
all over the city I search to settle
for a black haired blue eyed doll
sold by her father to buy food

Nothing exotic in Kerdassa
a baby inside on the mat
the air confiscated by a swath of black flies

Streets Are Endless Configurations

of sidewalks,
                a hill to climb up
creased with impromptu city peddlers,
                              incense 25 piasters.

Today termus beans floating in the water basin
in front of the woman
                who sits on silver bucket—knees apart,
her dress forms a hammock for sorting.

Across the street, the same nightgown dress
patterned spots
head bent low,
            touch braids to crossed knees
locked ankles rest a hand,
a palm begs for coins.

A woman's fingers glaze this pastry store window
a wonder from Santa's magic wand
           movement bends the elves to carve
a doll, a train, a horse that rocks
                  to carry western sky shining.
Her face turns to side
the black sweep of her dress retrieves dust
lashes winged   eyes open
an invitation
to where her knuckled fingers
              still glaze this scene.

From the Roof of 8 Salamlek Street

Framed in a flat rooftop
       crossword puzzle cables   step over
Below   traffic like threaded lanterns
       sounds sustain me
Above   a window   cornered
       half-shadow into someone's evening meal:
       white cheese, black olives, flat brown bread
            piled like a step pyramid
Overlooking the Saudi Embassy
       no line stretches the sidewalk
   except one man   a briefcase lingering
   in his arm

Garden City

Sun dispersed heat curves
inside Garden City streets

Three men inflate the collapsed tire
of a butagaz truck

Guards in stitched boots kick a plastic bottle
till a car catches its edge

In the corner flower shop
a man trims blossomed rose petals into buds

Cairo Walk

ربنا يخرب بيتك
"rabena yekhreb beitek"
(May god destroy your home)

perhaps her wind teased skirt,
                    chiffon in burgundy
or hair, curls and the sun's trick

intrigued this man into excitement
bringing to his lips a curse

عسل
"asel"
(honey)

        قشطة
        "eshta"
        (cream)

                شربات
                "sharbat"
                (wedding punch)

staccato
        an evanescent drill whispered into the ear

sensual is hair open, flamingo in sunlight
an ankle raffish
        like a mulberry leaf spinning

ربنا يخليني أتجوزك
"rabena yekhaliny atgouezek"
(May god let me marry you)

the request too quick
an improvisation
for a private prayer

Elegy for a Man Walking on Kasr el Aini Street

uneasily rendered this man will not forge the step   his foot
insists on the next centimeter   measures with meticulous
precision   juxtaposing of cane and two feet   writhing
his slit bouldered back   to approach this interceding
child mad dashing to a school gate   cracked bone hand
hollowed into the arc of a gripped cane   another
step repels an arm rupturing air   regrounding   his
head descends   balancing the seizure of his rocked plateau

Dust Bowl

"I saw a dead man on the street today."
How do you know?
                        a foot with centered skin folds
    hardened heel   stepped into sewer mud
                   then merged to this sidewalk

With gray wet dust
children drying
skin and hair matted down
the child made flatter
a face running after you
a hand pulling your clothes

A woman bares her breast
with a sound like an Arabian Oryx being roped
clutched scream cut short by tearing cloth
to yield purple shapes burned into a tornado's thrashing
upturned thunderclouds on her breast

Retrace these streets
destruct the heat
mid-summer sunstroke
you dehydrate into sweat
in your head the weight of a brick lightly thrown up
plucked by a man on top of a ladder
like some airborne piece of paper

Burden

Cantaloupes on cushioned head
Descend to indent palm

A *dikka* bench on nape of neck
Climb 6 flights

Cement blocks on single shouldered bones
Heave ship to land

Refrigerator on hump back
Glide through store

Garbage sacks on cracked knuckles
Lift rooftop to cart

Bags of oranges on arm's length
Sag sidewalk to street

Cone of falafel on fingertips
Cradle from kiosk to home

The Man Whose Ola Cart Fell Over

A man pulls his cart piled with clay olas
maneuvers the knotted traffic
olas for sale to contain cool water
quench the sand starched mouth

Futile to unlock this tongue—
I'm lost here
mazed into a pattern of textures and rhythms
snatched by the clutches of the tied bird of prey in the zoo
out of tune with the peacock caged in the pet store
stitched into the canvas of human sweat—
to divulge the secret of this magnet that draws us near

a reckless gesture stumbles into the ola cart
scatters clay shards
and continues

Garbage City

Mostly it's the little girls
                in dirt spotted
                  frilly dresses
and mostly
it's the older girls
        eager to shake your hand
on the mat sitting for Sunday school: to inspire cleanliness
                        a prize is given

But the intoxication of the city's garbage clings
and metro passengers step back.

Sorting through to find a shirt— salvaged
                      thrown into a barrel.
Later a can could be recycled,
          another barrel for the pigs' food.

If I throw away the green canvas bag with a broken
strap, will someone fix it?

Where is the dead sidewalk cat
           —fly eaten intestines— odor escaping?

Flattened tin: to create walls:
                home:
    a section for a cart or straw woven sack
           another smaller   for the family.

My husband and I argue.
When people visit he wants to show them everything.
I am defensive.
Embrace this too?

                  Shake a tree,
                          volcanic upsurge of flies.

I'd like to tuck this garbage city under
pretend my garbage dies in an incinerator
not return to life in Mustafa's home—my garbage man
elf-like in his green galabiya, rocking head
and crooked smiling.

V

Rubies

Why dreams blood colored
suggest sky colors
earth mixed with sea
to yellow green red of feast days
a thousand crowds picnic
among sidewalk grass.

Holidays are full of little girls in ruffled dresses, leather shoes,
pigtails and ribbons, socks with lace
growing up into tight dressed high heeled teenager
swinging her round of butt across Sunny's Supermarket
aware of her hair
swaying her back.

The fruit seller's son scratches his head,
stares at the daughter
light brown hair and blue shoes   clicked away
entering a crowded bathroom, the mirror catches
the whiff and curl adjusted midway to forehead,
a madonna Barbie, 100 pound price tag.

Crowned, adorned with Ken
providing French bedroom decor
the breeze's slight wisp into the stark undertone
of lace curtains drowned with yellow daisies
to undo the buttons.

Double Threads

In the Siwa Oasis, Abeela wants 35 pounds
for the woven straw sack

She knows the value of foreign desire
her bills a tight roll

But her sister Amer is still empty handed
henna scribbled palms

Veiled

muffled voice
is mother
bamboo shoot is woman
carved out   toned to
soft tune whistle
white glove touch
in sack light requiem

       tiptoed red heels   at the opera
                a ballet walker

       eyes dripped
              pharaonic lines perspiring
                  in black olive

inside breath is hot
boomeranging back

Given Sound

speak low
don't scream your words to heaven's clouds
it's men who raise voices
over a din of faces brushed into canvas wall
a woman soft whispers
undertoned to ears distracted by silence

Along the Nile Corniche

sounds swing shift in tone
stretched hands conspire
the wayward here
intersect
to jasmine necklaces
> *for the pretty lady*

leaves sift air
a breeze weaves branches
sheltering whispers
sugared hot tea
> *for the sweet lady*

a man gestures his voice
to stardom
claims his fortune
> *for the kind lady*

Mediterranean Beach

Sunglade palm trees
Oasis beach in El Arish
                         Mediterranean plush waves
                         embrace smooth down skin

      In Marsa Matruh the women swim
      clothes cling
                   cut tight
                   by water's edge
         skirts twist
                   turn mermaid ankles
         scarf riveted   rising

                         Other women boil water
                         hot tea for bare bellied men

Children streak the sand
                   gathering to the man
                   selling sesame sweets

The Roof Crumbles

for Lisa Suhair Majaj

pulverized to jagged
        one wall   one bed
        open to sunlight

The woman in a dark galabiya, veiled hair
        stands under the quarter roof
        eyes open and round like scarabs

planes dropping bombs,
running
        to quagmire and refugee camp

        now her hut overlooks the border
        mired with napalm

She turns to the single steel frame bed
notices the empty bucket rolled on its side
starts this day's walk to the one faucet

Incidents

Again explosions:
elevator door slam
bed shakes
cat scratching or the earth shifting us
Something expected today
arrives in business suit: "get out of my country or I'll kill you"

A cafe shouts its insides
of turkish coffee
spills the Tahrir Square sidewalk

A bomb camouflaging as a bus
scatters glass
"we're targets!" "we're targets!" a foreigner shrieks
and a man continues to sell newspapers

Assassination Attempt

Kiosk blown to shrapnel
ricochets the parking attendant
into car's headlight
glass sprinkles like snow
at the university gate an uncle catapulted
against wall's graying cement
his nephew chases a runaway 10 pound note

    Damascus Hospital, I cradle our newborn daughter
    wait for my husband to return with translated birth certificate
    my aunt chatters *when you have a child it makes you see*
        so far into the future

On the corner
my husband catches first claps
gunshots echoing explosions
he stands to steady the ground
till thunder's echo trails blood
streaks at entrance gate
the market nearby trembles with furor

Fraudulent Acts

to be walking on the Nile corniche
nostalgia bordered by sticky smog of polluted air
to hail a cab, negotiate a fare
         hold the silent facade   of being Egyptian
who impersonates
    walking through a Nubian village
people guess: "he's Egyptian you're Foreigner"
the waiter in Falfela taking me for a European woman

But once in Siwa a young man recognizes I am Coptic
"it was your eyes"
the first time I imagine my religion
        shadowed on my features
            like a palm tree carries
            its ripened yellow dates
Maggie tells me Copts have big round eyes, small chins
I search out faces   decipher the lines that draw us
At the spring fed pond near desert edge,
where soon an Italian company will build a luxury hotel
advertising the healing waters of Siwa,
a young boy assures "Copts are bad and must die"
                           taken to where

there was a woman who found herself drowning in the water while carrying her child. desperate because the child had not been baptized and death was near, she said in the name of the father and son and baptized the child herself in the sea's water. after she was rescued, she went to the church, but every time the priest lowered her child to the basin, the water dried up. three times this happened until the priest asked her if this child had ever been baptized before. the woman confessed and told him what had happened. and the priest said, God has accepted your baptism.

                    having carried
                    this story against so many doubts

"So you'll have to wear a veil"
a breath to inhale to explain
overlooking heads: anyone with uncovered hair now suspect
likely to be Coptic
taken for what   at the airport's glass enclosure
aren't you Egyptian why the passport stamped Tourist?

VI

From a Distance Born

for Celine

From a distance born
into snow wind
hazy sky moon drive to the hospital
for thirty-six hours
        your head a keen piercing
turning low inside me

      my body resists your entrance
clear dawn light
a display of rectangles
   the hospital building at right angles

each contraction spread thin like fish skin stretches over tabla
  to push you out only a pretense
into a round of unutterable consonants

From your father's hand pressed tight into mine
dark musk smell
        mixture of incense, coconut traced to
Aswan market street, dusk light
burlap bags rolled open: sassafras, hibiscus,
smell of peanuts roasted in sand
  a breath walking on the wind

a man sits at the marina's edge,
       his arm a seesaw on the *rebaba*
        music strung through water and sand
     catapults
        to a plateau of sounds

What can I give you here
I have been able to hold nothing
each year, I return to the moment of departure
a careening convulsion of fear
        shifting earth planes break apart to   isolation
a loss of chatter   uncles aunts cousins grandparents
unable to utter
  letters in arabic script to spellout
  home like an iceberg dissolving

the doctor's arrival with forceps
your father's voice, a command exerting you out into
                                        on my body
                                I lay my hand over you

The second night
        still awkwardly balanced
                        in my cradle hold
closed eyelids quiver with your mouth's movement
for a long time   you eat

finally taken to the nursery
ten minutes later, the nurse returns
        your face a reddened demand: hungry
                                        crying
out of my own desire for sleep I hold you
eyes intent on my face   dark
as if the night of our labor is still in them
    merging into black   I can't trace their circles
you turn away from my breast
only your eyes reach my face like a hung note
straining its pitch

at last you take two sips
then fall firmly asleep
having confirmed that crying will always lead
                                    to this place
you claim me for your own.

Homelands Amiss

A breeze of leaves surprises high wires
A breath of wind slips through an oasis of palm trees
                              some other place   simultaneous
                                                  movement
        where am I ever when I am here
        the way sun enters intrusive upon the skin

Yesterday my two year old daughter pursued her desire
for a walk to the park
"I looked both ways"   paying homage to family rules
"Over There" a neighbor shouts as our lungs search her out
over there a dozen hands would have held her still
questioning her to home quickly

This day in bird song passes, windy sun
and a humming quietness
                        yet early dawn a dog's barking awakens me
    back to Salamlek Street and the tribal disagreements of a dozen dogs
        I'm wary of overstepping their territory

        what am I doing here
        full of autumn's blood red foliage
        fading to a vague impression of itself

In the mall a young boy circles   calls for his mother
Shoppers maze in oblivious ears   till I intrude   a journey
                                            to some safety

Leap to Grasp

caught to land two feet on lowest bus step secured by massed puzzled
bodies twist like that game turn touching color circles till shapes insert
under twined into beneath this plump body decreases squeezes hunches
secures by these suffocations

Why not leave

clay cup hooked with a string— this for drink in summer heat
        the communal ola filled with water   resting on sidewalk
sweet potato unjoined to orange as butter cream steam—

                                                      evaporating
cymbals ring for a cup of licorice juice
from the man in pantaloons
        a sour taste— spit out

When I return— shreds in silk,
Bedouin needlepoint, a handmade rug   decorated by things
real Egyptians don't own
can't steal the sweet potato vendor
to take him back:
a clay statue

Upon Arriving

first thing I look for
is a middle eastern grocery store
even though I've had enough of
fava beans
and feta cheese

Back Porch

for T.J.

Rocked by the wind
urged by the hot sun
close to earth, color of wheat
slower, putting my mind
to the pace of a bird's song
my eyes to the distance of a cattail growing

I buy vegetables from the farmers
take back my first judgments
look again
let an extra hour slip by

Stop paddling
let the canoe drift   watch   fish spawning
turtles diving
hold a frog in my palm

I welcome the golden grey squirrels to my attic
let them live undisturbed and sit on my porch
watching the evening sun with me
as I trace the route of ants living under my window
while they carry their eggs, their dead
across the railing from one home to another

Utterances

tell three silent things

ال لغة / *el logha* / *language*
thoughts in Arabic
slipped into a school desk
my lips don't move
to make words in English

الحزن / *el hozn* / *sadness*
my father's face ashen gray
facing skylight sun window
eyes fixed to travel distance
the call from Egypt that his mother died

النفس / *el nafes* / *breath*
crouched under my parent's bed
a cupped hand
quieting the air from my nostrils
hiding from departure

three loud things

المهرجان /*el mahragan* / *festival*
music of tabla and oud chattering
twined conversations unaccented
the dabka circle spiraling
feet shuffled and stomping the ground

النرفزة / *eel narvaza* / *temper*
swearing in arabic a mad tirade
damn and the dog and hell and a donkey
my husband and children hear
syllables pound out like a shoe beating

أول يوم / *awel yom* / *first day*
my aunt's laughter calling to the sky
her feet slipping the moist ground
our walk across this park
a trail of falls into piles of snow

three eternal things

الفاضل / *el fadel* / *what remains*

the story of my uncle carving his name
at the peak of Khufu's pyramid

my grandmother's hand on my face to wake me
morning of our flight

smoothed mango pits held in jars of water
my mother and I waiting for sprouts

Pauline Kaldas was born in Egypt and immigrated to the United States in 1969. She is the author of *Letters from Cairo* and the co-editor of *Dinarzad's Children: An Anthology of Contemporary Arab American Fiction.* Her work has appeared in several journals and anthologies, and she was awarded a fellowship from the Virginia Commission for the Arts in Fiction. She teaches literature and creative writing at Hollins University.

Printed in the United States
66776LVS00008B/178-180

9 781933 456256